What's Wrong With the Name it and Claim it Gospel

John "BJ" Hall

Copyright © 1987 John "BJ" Hall. Revised 2004

All rights reserved.

ISBN-13:
978-1466415768

ISBN-10:
1466415762

DEDICATION

This book is dedicated to the memory of Rev. Harold Amos Hall who served faithfully in small town and rural churches for over forty years. Many of the churches he served as pastor were dying when he came and thriving when he went on to the next place of service. I learned much under the tutelage of this great man of God who sacrificially served in many cases where no one else would go. I am proud to be his son.

CONTENTS

	1 John 4:1 (KJV)	i
1	We have a problem	1
2	The Authority	13
3	The Materialism	16
4	The Revelation	19
5	Another Gospel	23
6	The Problem	29
7	The Consequences	40

"Beloved. Believe not every spirit, but try the spirits whether they are of God because many false prophets are gone out into the world."

1 John 4:1 (KJV)

Author's Preface

The purpose of this book is two-fold. That purpose is to expose false teaching and show what the Bible really says about those "teachings."

I want to make it clear from the beginning that I am not judging these teachers and their salvation. In fact I am convinced that some of their listeners have come to know Christ as personal Lord and Savior through the years. For this I am thankful. I am also convinced that many of these teachers started out with a pure heart and became enamored with corrupted understanding of the Word.

The problem that we are dealing with is one that has affected many people in a negative way. I have personally ministered to many people who have had their faith crushed by those who have told them that the only reason they were not healed, or their loved one died, was their lack of faith. I have ministered to those who have been told that going to the doctor or taking medication is an act of disbelief.

My desire is to educate pastors, teachers, and Bible students concerning these teachers and their teachings, some of which border on heresy.

This type of teaching comes from a misunderstanding of the true nature of our Lord and Savior, Jesus Christ and what He came to do in this world. They also spring from an exaggerated sense of the will of man as compared to the will of God.

It is my prayer that each reader of this book would examine his or her own beliefs in the light of God's Holy Word.

It really does matter what we believe and why we believe it.

John "BJ" Hall

1

WE HAVE A PROBLEM

Many of us have heard TV evangelists make statements such as this: "God's love and His will for you is to enjoy perfect health; He wants you to be rich; He owns the cattle on a thousand hills. Would an earthly millionaire make his own children eat poor food, wear shabby clothes, and ride in a broken down family car? Of course not! Neither will your heavenly Father give you anything but the very best! What is the desire of your heart? Name it, claim it by faith, and it is yours!"

Hobart Freeman (October l7, l920 - December, l984) was one who adhered to the same tenets. He was born in Ewing, Kentucky, grew up in St. Petersburg, Florida, and became a successful businessman, converted at the age of 31 into the Southern Baptist Church.

His theological background includes a Th.D. degree and a seminary professorship in Hebrew and Old Testament.

All this took place within about ten years of his conversion experience.

He left the seminary ranks and started a church of his own, the Faith Assembly, located in northeast Indiana. Among the beliefs he espoused was what is commonly called the gospel of guaranteed prosperity and health.

The November 23, 1984 issue of *Christianity Today* says, "According to Freeman's faith-formula theology, God is obligated to heal every sickness if a believer's faith is genuine. Faith must be accompanied by `positive confession,' meaning that believers must `claim' the healing by acknowledging that it has taken place."[1]

Freeman wrote in his book, "We must practice thought control. We must deliberately empty our minds of everything negative concerning the person, problem or situation confronting us."[2]

He taught that after healing is claimed, symptoms of illness or injury that remain are viewed as deception from the devil. When death occurs despite a positive confession, it is interpreted as discipline from God or a lack of faith.

This type of thinking is the same as other cult leaders like Victor Paul Wierwille of The Way International who died of an illness. Apparently something was wrong with his faith. Hobart Freeman also died of an illness that may have been medically treatable.

The saddest part is that it did not stop with Freeman. There have been over 100 members of Freeman's Church who have died as a result of his teachings. Numerous lawsuits have been filed, and parents convicted of child abuse.

The late Hobart Freeman said, "To claim healing for the body and then to continue to take medicine is not following our faith with corresponding action.... When genuine faith is present, it alone will be sufficient and will take the place of medicine and other needs,"[3]

Christians need to be careful and not fall into such shallow teachings. God never promised perfection in the here and now on planet Earth. Perfection for the believer is reserved for heaven.

Some call it the "prosperity gospel." This writer has spent an extensive amount of time examining the evidence and has personally listened to multiplied hours of the proponents of the doctrine. It has become evident that it is nothing less than what I will call EVANGELICAL HUMANISM.

It is important that we first establish certain definitions concerning humanism.

1. Humanism – A doctrine, set of attitudes, or way of life centered upon human interests or values.[4]
2. Secular Humanism – "noun [u] a set of beliefs which emphasize the importance of reason and of individuals rather than religion."[5] It builds its world view and understanding of reality on the natural not the supernatural, in particular declaring that man is the ultimate authority in all things. The common belief is that IF there is a God, He is irrelevant in the post modern era.
3. Christian Humanism – Human worth and dignity are affirmed through the Christian faith in one true and loving God who sent His Son to die on Calvary and save us from our sins, giving us eternal life by His resurrection.
4. Evangelical Humanism – Involves the idea of man's innate goodness. It is built upon the idea that low self-esteem is rampant and the root of almost all problems. Evangelical tradition is replaced by a new humanistic view of man. As Charles Capps, radio minister from England, Arkansas puts it, ". . . Jesus said 'ye are gods.' In other words, Adam was a god of the earth . . . Man was created . . . to be god over the earth. . ."[6] Kenneth Copland has said, "You don't have a God living in you; you ARE one!"[7] This doctrine tends to take away from the authority of Scripture and replace it with the authority of man's will, all of which are based on a few Scriptures pulled out of context and in most cases misinterpreted.

The Dictionary of Pentecostal and Charismatic Movements' article on "Positive Confession Theology" serves as both a documentation of the heretical teachings and the teachers of the word-faith movement, as well as some sound correction.

It identifies E.W. Kenyon as the founder, and men such as Kenneth Hagin, Kenneth Copeland, Charles Capps, Frederick K.C. Price, Robert Tilton, Earl Paulk, and others as his disciples.

The article states that the "theological claims, while based on faulty presuppositions, have a universal appeal" as they feed the natural fallen nature of man.

The article points out that "the Rhema interpretation is their biased selection of biblical passages, often without due regard to their context. This approach not only does violence to the text but forces the New Testament linguistic data into artificial categories that the Bible authors themselves could not affirm."[8]

Faith-healer evangelist W.V. Grant sent out an interesting letter here. There was a cap pasted on the letter, very similar to a toothpaste tube cap. The personalized form letter says that Grant feels so close to them in the Spirit and that right now God wants to do something powerful in their lives.

But, first he wants to tell them about some anointing oil that God had him set aside on his "altar three weeks ago." By touching the bottle lid and saying "a prayer over it" one will get the "blessing started." Then send the bottle lid back with a requested $50.00, and Grant will rush the precious anointing oil back to generate a miracle.[9]

Apparently, there needs to be more exposure. Christ and His cause can never be substituted for humanistic practices like this.

---

[1] CHRISTIANITY TODAY, (November 23, 1984)
[2] Hobart Freeman POSITIVE THINKING AND CONFESSION (Faith Publications) np, nd
[3] Ibid
[4] Webster's New Collegiate Dictionary, 1977 ed., s.v. "humanism."
[5] Cambridge Advanced Learner's Dictionary, http://dictionary.cambridge.org/, s.v. "secular humanism"
[6] Charles Capps, personal letter, June 4, 1982
[7] Kenneth Copeland, "The Forces of Love." Tape #BCC-56, Broken Arrow, OK
[8] DICTIONARY OF PENTECOSTAL AND CHARISMATIC MOVEMENTS, 1988, pp. 718-720.
[9] W.V. Grant, SOLICITATION LETTER

2
THE AUTHORITY

Those who proclaim Evangelical Humanism seem to be able to find ample scriptural evidence that this is God's will for all believers. For example, Oral Roberts is fond of quoting III John 2, "Beloved, I wish above all things that thou mayest prosper and be in health, even as thy soul prospereth" (KJV). The Dake's annotated reference Bible is an important reference work for the Evangelical Humanist. This Bible has in its margin the following commentary on this verse:

> "If any one of these blessings (material prosperity, bodily healing and health, and soul salvation) was not the will of God, would it be the wish of this most beloved apostle? If such blessings are the will of God for one man, they are for all men alike who will have faith for them, because in the Gospel there is no respect of persons."[1]

This is not only a major misinterpretation but a misapplication of the verse. Actually it is not a promise at all but a "wish" from John, the writer, to Gaius that this letter might find him well and in good health. It is used in much the same way that we often begin a letter to a friend or loved one, "I hope you are doing well."

The verse that we find in the King James Version should be translated. The Greek preposition PERI is not "above" but "concerning" or "about." John is not saying that prosperity and wealth should be considered not as the greatest gifts of life.

The Greek word "prosper" is EUODOUSTHAI, the present infinitive of EUODOO which literally means to have a good journey, or a safe journey through life. That is how it is used in Romans 1:10. In 1 Corinthians 16:2 it is used in regard to the giving of benevolence to the church. The idea of wealth is entirely missing from the word for "prosper."

Another passage often used is John 15:7b, ". . . ye shall ask what ye will, and it shall be done unto you" (KJV) Concerning this verse, Dake says:

> "The promise is "ask what YE WILL." (his emphasis) plainly teaching that answered prayer is up to the child of God as to what he wants. This is in perfect harmony with promises of both testaments. A true Christian can *get anything* (my emphasis) he wants as well as what he needs. . .A prayer saying, 'If it be Thy will' concerning anything God has already promised, and therefore has already made clear that it is His will, providing we ask in faith, nothing wavering, is really a prayer of unbelief. It is like saying, 'I know You have already promised and You have made it very clear by Your Word that it is Your will but do You really mean what You say? Are You a truthful God or not? Can we depend upon what You say?' We insult God by constantly questioning his will that is already revealed by His word..."[2]

A.T. Robertson said, "This astounding command and promise ... is not without conditions and limitations. It involves such intimate union and harmony with Christ that nothing will be asked out of accord with the mind of Christ and so of the Father."[3] This is in contrast to the statement that any "true Christian can get what he wants." It is not ethical to use only part of a promise verse without consideration for the "conditions and limitations" on that promise.

This all leads to an attitude of self importance and authority that is far beyond what Scripture provides. Daisy Osborn, wife of "international evangelist" T.L. Osborn, said, ". . . decide what you want and then tell God that you want it . . . Your will becomes God's will . . . because you are His representative on earth."[4]

It is important here to note that authority comes from some sort of sinless perfection..Joyce Meyer declared on tape that she no longer is a sinner:

> "I'm going to tell you something folks, I didn't stop sinning until I finally got it through my thick head I wasn't a sinner anymore. And the religious world thinks that's heresy and they want to hang you for it. But the Bible says that I'm righteous and I can't be righteous and be a sinner at the same time ... All I was ever taught to say was, 'I'm a poor, miserable sinner.' I am not poor, I am not miserable and I am not a sinner. That is a lie from the pit of hell. That is what I was and if I still am then Jesus died in vain. Amen?"[5]

The Apostle John says, "If we claim to be without sin, we deceive ourselves and the truth is not in us" (1 John 1:8). It is Christ's righteousness imparted to us, not ours, that makes us righteous.

---

[1] Finis Jennings Dake, DAKE'S ANNOTATED REFERENCE BIBLE, (Dake Bible Sales, Inc.: Lawrenceville Georgia, 1981), p. 282
[2] Ibid, s.v. "ASK WHAT YE WILL," p. 121
[3] A.T. Robertson, WORD PICTURES IN THE NEW TESTAMENT, (Broadman Press: Nashville), Vol. 5, p. 259, 1932
[4] KNYD-FM, Dr. Daisey Osborn, "Women's Voice", 20 July 1987
[5] Joyce Meyers, WHAT HAPPENED FROM THE CROSS TO THE THRONE?, (Audio tape that is mysteriously no longer available)

3

THE MATERIALISM

On July 21, 1987, Charles Capps, another of this doctrines main promoters said, "Now faith is the substance of THINGS" (emphasis his). He did not at any time complete the verse or even the remainder of the phrase found in Hebrews 11:1. The emphasis of His entire message was that it is God's will for us to have an abundance of "THINGS" in this life.[1]

Further, Charles Capps tells you how to acquire it. In an Occult *spell casting style*, he says, "For Material Needs Confess These Three Times a Day Until They're Manifest."[2]

David Wilkerson has said:

> "There is an evil wind . . . blowing into God's house, deceiving multitudes of God's chosen people . . . It is a scriptural take-off on Napoleon Hills' book, THINK AND GROW RICH.
>
> This perverted gospel seeks to make gods of people. They are told, "Your destiny is in the power of your mind. Whatever you can conceive is yours. Speak it into being. Create it by a positive mind set. Success, happiness, perfect health is all yours—if you will only use your mind creatively. Turn your dreams into reality by using mind power."[3]

One theological model gives primary attention to a belief that God has set certain laws or principles in the universe, including laws on health and wealth. According to this view all the child of God has to do is learn the principles that apply in a given situation and then put them into operation.[4]

One of the leaders of the positive confession (evangelical humanism) movement writes: "This is not theory. It is fact. It is spiritual law. It works every time it is applied correctly . . . You set them [spiritual laws] in motion by the word of your mouth . . . everything you say will come to pass."[5]

It also seems that Jesus is obligated by the evangelical humanist to teach this doctrine. Another leader writes: "Then He [Jesus] said, 'if anybody anywhere will take these four steps or will put these four principles into operation, they will always receive whatever they want from Me or from God the Father.'"[6]

This author and his family have been in conversations in which the evangelical humanists pressed their beliefs. His wife and mother-in-law were at a laundromat in Gore, Oklahoma. The woman that owned the laundry overheard them talking about their father/husband who was in critical condition in the intensive care unit at Muskogee General Hospital in Muskogee, Oklahoma. The woman interrupted their conversation to tell them that all they had to do was say that their father/husband was well and he would be well.

After a short time this same woman was complaining about the electric bill for her driers and said, "You know, it's illegal, but I had to turn the timers back on those driers so people would only get fifteen cents worth of drying time for a quarter." Then in the same conversation she bragged about how much she had been blessed because of her faith.[7]

This writers family did not take the advice of this lady. They prayed that God's will be done. Coney Books came home from the hospital and had three of the best years of his life before finally going home to be with the Lord.

A young man in Depew, Oklahoma told this writer about an incident that took place when he was a young Christian. A woman in the church he was attending said to him, "God is ashamed of you because your tennis shoes are so old . . . If you were walking in faith you would not be wearing tennis shoes like that . . . It's too bad that you only have the faith to drive a Volkswagen . . . I don't know about you but I'm going to drive a Cadillac . . ."[8]

---

[1] KNYD-FM, Charles Capps, 21 July 1987
[2] Charles Capps, GOD'S CREATIVE POWER, (np: England, Arkansas), p. 17, nd
[3] David Wilkerson, A PROPHECY WALL OF FIRE, (World Challenge: Lindale, TX), nd., p. 15, nd.
[4] Dr. James Bjornstad, "What is Behind the Prosperity Gospel?" MOODY MONTHLY, November, 1986, p. 19.
[5] Charles Capps, THE TONGUE—A CREATIVE FORCE. (np: England, Arkansas), p. 23, 131, 132, nd.
[6] Kenneth E. Hagin, BIBLE STUDY FAITH COURSE, (np: Broken Arrow, OK), p. 104, nd,
[7] Connie Hall, et.al., personal conversation held June 17, 1987, Gore, OK
[8] Jim Campbell, personal interview held 17 July 1987 in Mr. Campbell's home

4

THE REVELATION

A third ethical problem with this doctrine has to do with revelation. Is the Bible the final authoritative source for Christian living? Is the Bible the "complete" revelation of God for the world? Those who promote evangelical humanism seem to be saying that God is still inspiring Scripture through them today. J. Rodman Williams explained what amounts to a "progressive" or "continuing" revelation:

> "For in the Spirit the present fellowship is as much the arena of God's vital presence as anything in the Biblical account. Indeed, in the light of what we may learn from this past witness, and take to heart, we may expect new things to occur in our day and days to come."[1]

Once we see Scripture as less than the final inerrant authority for faith and practice, we have opened the doors to theological chaos. Anyone or everyone can claim to be speaking God's revelation.

This may be seen in the plea by Oral Roberts in a letter to His "partners" in September of 1980. The first few paragraphs of the letter have an almost threatening tone as Mr. Roberts tells his "partners" about the consequences of disobedience. ". . . I brought upon myself most of the bad things that happened to me. By my disobedience to the Lord . . ." Then He begins to tell them of an "experience" in which he saw a 900 foot tall Jesus.

> "Jesus Christ . . . I have only seen Jesus once before, but here I was face to face with the King of Kings . . . Jesus looked straight at me and said, '. . . When I speak to your partners and they obey me, it will not be difficult to finish this (referring to the City of Faith Hospital which never became a viable hospital and later was sold) . . . Partner, Jesus let me know in unmistakable terms that OBEDIENCE IS THE KEY, AND THAT DISOBEDIENCE WILL DEFEAT US, AND HIS WORK (original emphasis) . . . Then Jesus said, 'Tell your partners to obey what I speak . . and I will send My angels to stop the devil from stealing their money . . "[2]

The implication in the letter is to fail to send money to Oral Roberts is direct disobedience of Jesus. He said, "My word is good and I give it to you, but I want you to go beyond my word, to JESUS' WORD; to obey Him"[3]

Joyce Meyer advocates peculiar and unbiblical manifestations at church gatherings, and attributes them to the power of God. She proclaims,

> "You gotta come on out in the deep....Oh, I think that word's anointed right now. Deeeep!!! Mmmmmm! One lady was in a conference recently in St. Louis, and she said "I am telling you, every time you said the word "deep" the fire of God hit me in the pit of my guts." The lady, she kept falling out of her chair and being on the floor, you know? And she said later, "every time you said 'deeeeep' it was like I just couldn't stay in my chair!"[4]

Although there is no biblical precedent, she makes the assertion that angels tell her what to preach:

> Now spirits don't have bodies, so we can't see them. Okay? There probably is, I believe there is, and I

certainly hope there is (sic) several angels up here this morning that are preaching with me. I believe that right before I speak some anointed statement to you, that one of them bends over and says in my ear what I'm supposed to say to you.[5]

She goes on to promote the superstitious belief that certain kinds of jewelry attract evil spirits:

> There are many different signs and emblems that people wear as jewelry that are straight from the devil, and they absolutely do not know it, and I'm quite sure there are going to be people here today that probably even have some of these things in your possession. You may even be wearing one. And what they do is they draw evil spirits.[6] (sic)

In lieu of the biblical admonition to test everything by the objective Word of God (1 Thess. 5:21; 2 Tim. 3:16), Meyer further asserts that God would never allow her to fall into error. Turning instead to her subjective feelings she says,

> I am going to tell you something right now. I no more believe that my God is going to let me stand around and believe a lie than I believe that I am going to turn green in the next two minutes. God is my source and He loves me and I am after God with my whole heart. And if I am accidentally, or any other way, getting into error, I am going to have a bell go off on the inside of me that is going to be so loud that not only am I going to hear it, but so is everybody else.[7]

Despite what Meyer's feelings tell her, Scripture says otherwise. The apostle Peter is a constant reminder of our proclivity for committing error, and demonstrated, for example, by Christ's rebuking of Peter for attempting to deter Him from His mission (Matt. 16:22-23; Mark 8:31-33), and later by being publicly rebuked by the apostle Paul for yielding to the pressure of the Judaizers (Gal. 2:11-21). Were it not possible for Meyer to fall into deception and error, Scripture's repeated warnings (e.g., Matt. 24:4-5; Acts 20:28-31; Gal. 1:6-9; 2 Thess. 2:1-3; 2 Tim. 4:3-4; 2 Peter 2:1-3) would be meaningless.

Also problematic are some of Meyer's beliefs regarding spiritual warfare. According to her, for instance, *generational* spirits supposedly torment families for generations with specific sins, and she even believes that a demon of lust torments her family. On one occasion she says,

> I told you that there was a spirit of incest in my family bloodline....And the thing that I want you to understand today is when there's a spirit like that in a bloodline, until some person believes on Jesus and takes the blood of Jesus and draws it across that natural bloodline, that devastation goes on for generations and generations....Well see, my father's grandfather had problems and so his father had problems and so my dad had problems and so I had problems and so if I wouldn't have stood and believed Jesus, my kids would have had problems and their kids would have had problems and so on and so on.[8]

Though a quick surface reading of the scriptures used to justify this doctrine might say that this doctrine is ethical, in fact these scriptures do not do so. All of them are pulled out of their context and stretched beyond reason in order to support a preconceived notion.

---

[1] Williams, J. Rodman, ERA OF THE SPIRIT, (Plainfield, N.J.: Logos International), pp. 17, 22., 1971
[2] Oral Roberts, Partnership letter, September 16, 1980
[3] Ibid
[4] Joyce Meyer, GO TO THE UPPER ROOM AND WAIT (Audiotape 6).
[5] Joyce Meyer, *Witchcraft & Related Spirits* (Audiotape, Part 1).
[6] Ibid
[7] Ibid
[8] Joyce Meyer, *Trophies of God's Grace* (Audiotape, Part 1).

5

ANOTHER GOSPEL

The issues we are dealing with are not light in nature. They go to the very core of our understanding of the atonement on the cross. Every cult and pseudo-Christian sect disparages the cross. An enemy of the cross is one who even suggests that Jesus Christ's sacrifice on the cross was insufficient for salvation. Anyone who disparages the cross is teaching another gospel. The destiny of such teachers is destruction (Philippians 3:19). Based upon Christ's atonement for their sins, Christians are not going to hell. Therefore, no enemy of the cross can be a brother in Christ.

This false teaching often leads to others false teachings with even more devastating results. For example, Jim Bakker believes all who died in the Holocaust are now in heaven regardless of whether or not they believed in Christ. The former pastor and leader of the PTL ministry told Larry King in a January 25, 2000 interview on CNN's Larry King Live broadcast that he believes "every person who died in the Holocaust is in heaven." King asked, "What you're saying, in a sense, is you don't have to believe in Christ to go to heaven...?" Bakker replied, "I believe that decision is in God's hands, not mine." King responded, "If they all died Jews or many, most died Jews, then they're in heaven?" Bakker replied, "That's right." While the tragedy of the Holocaust is a prime example of suffering and a reprehensible picture of the sinfulness of mankind, in no way do those who have rejected Christ as their Savior gain entrance into eternal glory with the Father, because of the fact that they have suffered greatly. Thousands of people of all nationalities have suffered and are currently suffering at the hands of oppressors. Yet their suffering does not allow automatic access to heaven. Such faulty theology must be rejected. Man can only be assured of heaven and a right relationship with God by personally believing that Jesus Christ died for him and that He rose again as a perfect substitute on his behalf.[1]

Bishop Carlton D. Pearson has written:

> A careful study of early church history will show that the doctrine of universal restoration was the prevailing doctrine of the Primitive Christian Church. The so-called "Doctrine of Inclusionism" or as some call it, the 'Theory of Universal Reconciliation' maintains that Christ's crucifixion and death on Calvary accomplished its purpose of reconciling all mankind to God. The death of Christ made it possible for God to accept sinful man, and that He has, in fact, done so. Consequently, whatever separation there is between man and the benefits of God's grace is subjective in nature and exists only in man's mind and unregenerate spirit. The message man needs to hear then, is not that he simply has a suggested opportunity for salvation, but that through Christ he has, in fact, already been redeemed to God and that he may enjoy the blessings that are already his through Christ.[2]

Kenneth Hagin has written:

> "Did you ever stop and think about it; salvation belongs to the sinner. Jesus already has bought the salvation of the worst sinner, just as He did for us. That's the reason he told us to go tell the sinner the Good News; go tell sinners they have been reconciled to God. But we never really told them that. We've told them God's mad at them and that He's counting up everything they've done wrong. Yet, the Bible says God isn't holding anything against the sinner! God says he's canceled it out."[3]

"Dad" Hagin goes on to say:

> "There is no sin problem, there is a sinner problem. Get the sinner to Jesus, and that cures the problem. Yes, that's a little different from what people have been taught, but it's what the Bible says. The sinner doesn't know what belongs to him, so it won't do him any good...."[4]

Several of these teachers have a twisted view of what Christ did on the cross:

> "Do you think that the punishment for our sin was to die on a cross? If that were the case, the two thieves could have paid our price. No, the punishment was to go into hell itself and to serve time in hell separated from God."[5]

> "Ladies and gentlemen, the serpent is a symbol of Satan. Jesus Christ knew the only way he would stop Satan was by becoming one in nature with him. You say, "What did you say? What blasphemy is this?" No, you hear this! He did not take my sin; He became my sin"[6]

> "When Jesus cried, "It is finished!" He was not speaking of the plan of redemption. There were still three days and nights to go through before He went to the throne. He was referring to the Abrahamic Covenant. Jesus' death on the cross was only the beginning of the complete work of redemption."[7]

> "The righteousness of God was made to be sin. He accepted the sin nature of Satan in His own spirit. And at that moment that He did so He cried, `My God, My God, Why hast thou forsaken me?' You don't know what happened at the cross. Why do you think Moses, upon instruction of God, raised the serpent upon that pole instead of a lamb? That use to bug me. I said, `Why in the world would you want to put a snake up there - the sign of Satan? Why didn't you put a lamb on that pole?' And the Lord said, `Because it was a sign of Satan that was hanging on the cross.' He (Jesus) said, `I accepted in my own spirit, spiritual death, and the light was turned off.'"[8]

Joyce Meyer assertions are not unlike those of other leading Word of Faith proponents who also believe Christ's death on the cross was not sufficient to atone for our sins, and that His work of redemption was completed by suffering in hell and being born again. She wrote:

> During that time He entered hell, where you and I deserved to go (legally) because of our sin....He paid the price there....no plan was too extreme...*Jesus paid* on the cross and in hell....God rose up from His throne and said to demon powers tormenting the sinless Son of God, "Let Him go." Then the resurrection power of Almighty God went through hell and filled Jesus....He was resurrected from the dead **the first born-again man.**[9] (emphasis in original)

Again Carlton Pearson has written:

> It may appear to us that when a person seems not to respond to a particular altar call or doesn't seem to accept Christ as or when we offer Him does not necessarily signify that they have rejected Him outright, though it feels to us like they have.
>
> If you look at it another way, it may only be possible for believers to actually reject Jesus. How can you reject something you've never realized or actualized? How can you reject something that is not real to you?
>
> In one sense, it may be almost impossible to reject something or someone you don't believe in or have never personally experienced. You can't, in reality, reject a thing unless you believe the thing exists, or have in some tangible or meaningful way experienced it and then choose not to accept it.[10]

If this teaching is true, then Jesus Himself has done a horrible injustice to the world. He commanded all of us to go into all the world and preach the Gospel:

> [18] And Jesus came and spake unto them, saying, All power is given unto me in heaven and in earth. [19] Go ye therefore, and teach all nations, baptizing them in

the name of the Father, and of the Son, and of the Holy Ghost: ²⁰ Teaching them to observe all things whatsoever I have commanded you: and, lo, I am with you alway, *even* unto the end of the world. Amen. Matt 28:18-20 (KJV)

⁸ But ye shall receive power, after that the Holy Ghost is come upon you: and ye shall be witnesses unto me both in Jerusalem, and in all Judaea, and in Samaria, and unto the uttermost part of the earth. Acts 1:7-8 (KJV)

If as Bishop Pearson states, "<u>You can't, in reality, reject a thing unless you believe the thing exists, or have in some tangible or meaningful way experienced it and then choose not to accept it</u>", then to go and take the chance on them rejecting Christ would be an act of condemnation to them. What a cruel hoax we would have been foisting on the world for the past 2000 years.

The teachers of this movement emphasize the "spiritual" death of Christ almost to the exclusion of His "physical" death. The problem with this is simply that it is unbiblical. The Bible's emphasis is on the physical death of Christ, not the spiritual. The teaching of scripture is: "Without shedding of blood (physical), is no remission" (Hebrews 9:22, parenthesis mine).

As regarding Christ's words, "It is finished", the word in the Greek is TETELISTAI and is rendered "to bring to an end" or "paid for in full."[11] What Christ was saying was that the work of redemption (paying for sin and securing salvation) was complete. If Christ did anything else beyond "It is finished," in order to pay for sin, something is added to His completed work. This is what the Word-Faith teachers have done when they teach that salvation was completed in hell, after Christ died on the cross!

On what Scripture do these teachers base their doctrine of the spiritual death of Christ? Most of them point to Psalm 22:1 where the Psalmist cried out "My God, My God, Why hast thou forsaken me?" Jesus, of course, uttered these words on the cross in fulfillment of the Psalmist's prophecy (Mark 15:34).

However, when reading Psalm 22, it is seen that God never abandoned the Psalmist (see 22:19, 22, 23, 24). In other psalms, we discover the Psalmist is always feeling like God had abandoned him when God had not. He seems to be saying, "God, where are you when I need you?" But in Psalm 22, David is merely expressing how he feels, rather than the idea of God really abandoning him.

Jesus, in his human nature, while on the cross, as He looks into the cup of death, expresses the very same feeling or emotion as did David. God never abandoned Christ on the cross. Rather, God turned His back to what was on Jesus, namely sin. Jesus was man's sin-bearer, but He was not polluted with man's sin-nature and the nature of Satan as the Word-Faith teacher's claim.

Finally, did Christ die spiritually? The answer is no, at least not in the way the leaders of this movement teach! The Bible does not teach that Jesus died spiritually. As a matter of fact, the Bible teaches just the opposite.

In I Peter 3:18, Peter states that Christ was "Put to death in the flesh, but quickened (made alive) by the Spirit." This does not mean that He was once dead spiritually and now He is alive spiritually, or by the Spirit.

In conclusion, if what the Word-Faith teacher's claim regarding the atonement of Christ is true, then one will have to rewrite the words of Christ on the cross. For instance, instead of saying "It is finished," Christ should have explained Himself by saying, "I'm not talking about the plan of salvation, but I'm talking about the Abrahamic covenant." Instead of Christ saying to the thief on the cross, "Today you will be with Me in Paradise," He should have said, "Today you will be with Me suffering in hell." Instead of saying, "Father, into Thy hands I commend My spirit," He should have said, "Satan, into your hands I commend My spirit."

It has not been an easy task to write this work. This writer has never been one to publicly criticize others in the ministry. He takes very seriously the sanctions in the Scripture against those who judge others and those who would cause harm to "God's anointed."

However, after extensive study into the theology of the evangelical humanists and comparing them to what the Scripture really says, this writer is compelled to expose these grievous errors so that others will not fall into their trap. He would only ask that you prayerfully consider what you have read and that you compare these teachings to God's Holy Word.

This writer is not making a judgment as to the salvation of these teachers. He is rather doing as the Scripture so clearly commands.

---

[1] FOUNDATION MAGAZINE, Fundamental Evangelistic Association, Los Osos, (Mar-Apr 2000, p. 46)
[2] Bishop Carlton D. Pearson JESUS: THE SAVIOR OF THE WORLD (The Gospel of Inclusion), http://www.myfaith.com/carlton-pearson-inclusion.htm
[3] Kenneth E. Hagin, Sr. "The Authority of The Believer", (np, nd)
[4] Ibid
[5] Frederick K.C. Price, *Ever Increasing Faith Messenger*, June 1990, p. 7
[6] Benny Hinn, Benny Hinn broadcast on TBN, December 15, 1990
[7] Kenneth Copeland, "Jesus - Our Lord of Glory", *Believer's Voice of Victory*, April, 1982, p. 3
[8] Kenneth Copeland, *What Happened From the Cross to the Throne?* cassette tape, Kenneth Copeland Ministries, parenthesis mine
[9] Meyer, THE MOST IMPORTANT DECISION YOU WILL EVER MAKE: A COMPLETE AND THOROUGH UNDERSTANDING OF WHAT IT MEANS TO BE BORN AGAIN (Tulsa: Harrison House, 1991), pp. 35-36, The 1996 version of this booklet contains slightly different wording, but essentially the same message
[10] Bishop Carlton D. Pearson JESUS: THE SAVIOR OF THE WORLD (The Gospel of Inclusion), http://www.myfaith.com/carlton-pearson-inclusion.htm
[11] VINE'S EXPOSITORY DICTIONARY OF OLD AND NEW TESTAMENT WORDS, s.v. "tetelistai"

6

THE PROBLEM

One might ask, "What is the ethical problem of living this kind of lifestyle?" First, it is of utmost importance in the household of faith that we use ethical means of interpretation of God's word. It is wrong to read into the Bible a preconceived notion based on incomplete passages and then to proclaim that notion as a valid doctrine. This has been practiced in virtually every area by those who are promoting evangelical humanism.

Such passages as Luke 6:24,25a, Luke 16:13, Matthew 6:19, Matthew 13:22, 1 Timothy 6:4, and James 2:6 are ignored or treated lightly by these teachers. II Peter 1:20, 21 plainly says, "[20] Knowing this first, that no prophecy of the scripture is of any private interpretation. [21] For the prophecy came not in old time by the will of man: but holy men of God spake *as they were* moved by the Holy Ghost." (KJV) The Amplified Bible put it this way, "[yet] first [you must] understand this, that no prophecy of Scripture is [a matter] of any personal or private or special interpretation (loosening, solving)."[1]

J.B. Phillips interpreted this verse like this, "But you must understand this at the outset, that no prophecy of scripture arose from an individual's interpretation of the truth." No matter which interpretation of the passage you have the effect is the same for those who proclaim this "gospel." Using a portion of a verse as a prosperity proof text may satisfy the followers of these new "prophets," but people who are serious about the scriptures find some serious errors in the way the texts are interpreted.[2]

For example, Kenneth Copeland says that angels will bring your new riches to you, He uses a portion of Psalm 103:20 ". . . the . . . angels . . . hearken to the Word of God."[3] He goes on to say that what they are hearkening to is our voices as we claim what we want.

The actual verse in its context is, "**20** Bless the LORD, ye his angels, that excel in strength, that do his commandments, hearkening unto the voice of his word. **21** Bless ye the LORD, all *ye* his hosts; *ye* ministers of his, that do his pleasure. **22** Bless the LORD, all his works in all places of his dominion: bless the LORD, O my soul." (KJV)

These verses say NOTHING about saints commanding angels. It is an admonition to all to hear and obey the words of the Lord, not the words of man. It teaches that angels obey God's commands to carry out His will. The context clarifies the verse further. Verse twenty is related to the fact that "the Lord has established His throne in the heavens; and His sovereignty rules over all" (v 19) and the angelic hosts "serve Him, doing His will. (v. 21).

Kenneth Hagin has written, ""[Man] was created on terms of equality with God, and he could stand in God's presence without any consciousness of inferiority...God made us as much like Himself as possible...He made us the same class of being that He is Himself...Man lived in the realm of God. He lived on terms equal with God...[The] believer is called Christ...That's who we are; we're Christ"[4]

Second, it is unethical to build a doctrine on the teachings of a man like Napoleon Hill, who states in his own book that the book was written in consultation with great men of the past that were long deceased at the time.[5] Some of Mr. Hills quotes sound like they were taken from the same playbook as the Evangelical Humanists. For example:

> "The starting point of all achievement is desire. Keep this constantly in mind. Weak desires bring weak results, just as a small amount of fire makes a small amount of heat."
>
> "Ideas... they have the power…"
>
> "Think and grow rich."

> "The sixth sense defies description! It cannot be described to a person who has not mastered the other principles of this philosophy, because such a person has no knowledge and no experience with which the sixth sense may be compared. Understanding the sixth sense comes only by meditation through mind development from within.
>
> "After you have mastered the principles described in this book, you will be prepared to accept as truth a statement which may, otherwise, be incredible to you, namely:
>
> *"Through the aid of the sixth sense, you will be warned of impending dangers in time to avoid them and notified of opportunities in time to embrace them* (emphasis his).
>
> "There comes to your aid and to do your bidding, with the development of the sixth sense, a 'guardian angel' who will open to you at all times the door to the temple of wisdom."[6]

Third, Jesus never asked for an offering from His audiences but in fact lived a meager lifestyle among the common people of Israel. Christ resisted the temptation to materialism as he refused to make stones into bread in the wilderness. (Matthew 4:1-4). He said to one who would follow him, ". . . Foxes have holes, and birds of the air have nests; but the Son of man hath not where to lay His head." Luke 9:58 (KJV)

If it were God's will for all believers to be "successful" why did He tell the rich young ruler to go and sell everything he had and give it to the poor, and then to come and follow Jesus? It was Jesus who said, "Woe unto you that are rich! for ye have received your consolation." Luke 6:24 (KJV)

Did He not call several of His apostles away from successful fishing businesses? Didn't Jesus ask Peter if he loved Him more than "these?" Why was it that when Paul went to Rome; he didn't ride first class? Did Paul not understand what the scripture said? Paul said, "Charge them that are rich in this world, that they be not high-minded, nor trust in uncertain riches, but in the living God, who giveth us richly all things to enjoy" I Timothy 6:17 (KJV). These are just a few of the questions that come to mind when one thinks about the ethics of the prosperity gospel or evangelical humanism.

Finally, "name it and claim it" theology is an American phenomenon that doesn't sell with Christians in other countries. They don't have the money to buy in. American Christians have much for which to thank God. Ingenuity and hard work do pay off in our economic system, and many wealthy believers are balancing the spiritual and material life to the glory of God; However others seem to be consumed by the quest for prosperity.

Jim and Tammy Bakker had their mansion and all their other possessions and they continued to plead for more donations so that they could "do the work of the Lord." Richard Roberts built a mansion in Tulsa and his father pleads for his life to raise eight million dollars. Remember that most of the contributors to these evangelical humanists are "little old ladies on a pension." After his release from prison Jim Bakker wrote a book entitled "I Was Wrong."

Other Pentecostal and Charismatic scholars have written in-depth correctives to this harmful teaching. This is significant as none of the word-faith teachers claim to be scholars or well-trained theologically. Many times they admit this and even foolishly ridicule those who have a depth of scholarship.

The Bible is very clear that those who become teachers have a much greater responsibility. They are to be well grounded in sound doctrine. (Colossians 2:6-7; Titus 1:9; Titus 2:1; 1 Timothy 3:1-3, 4:6; 2 Timothy 4:1-4; James 3:1).

Dr. Charles Farah, Jr. was Professor of Theology and Historical Studies at Oral Roberts University and wrote an excellent article for *Pneuma: The Journal of the Society for Pentecostal Studies* titled, "A Critical Analysis: The "Roots and Fruits" of Faith-Formula Theology" (Spring, 1981, pp. 3-21).

He summarizes his article by noting, "The movement uses Gnostic hermeneutical principles and displaces contextual scientific exegesis. It shares many of the goals of present day humanism, particularly in regards to the creaturely comforts. It is, in fact, a burgeoning heresy"[7]

A more recent article in *Pneuma*, "Cultic Origins of Word-Faith Theology Within the Charismatic Movement", was written by H. Terris Newman, Bible professor at Southeastern College of the Assemblies of God. Newman adds Paul Yonggi Cho, Norman Vincent Peale and Robert Schuller to the list of word-faith teacher who reflect more Mind-Science "theology" than Biblical truth.

He concludes, "In view of the fact of the cultic origins of the health and wealth gospel, its heretical Christology, it's devastating effects on human lives and the false portrayal of Christianity it presents to the world, this paper is a call to the wider evangelical community also to engage in an apologetic that will distinguish the gospel of Jesus Christ from those who indeed propagate a different gospel."[8]

This writer believes that the basis for this doctrine is the lie that the serpent told Adam and Eve in the garden, "For God doth know that in the day ye eat thereof, then your eyes shall be opened, and ye shall be as gods, knowing good and evil" Genesis 3:5 (KJV). Many false prophets have proclaimed this same message. The Mormons believe that "God was once a man like we are, and we shall one day be gods like him." Now these new prophets have brought this pagan idea into the household of faith where they tell us that we are already gods, and that whatever we say will come true whether it is good or bad.

If their doctrine were true and they really believed it, why do those who preach it still have to beg for money on every program? If it is true, why do they still have to use Madison Avenue methods to raise funds? The obvious answer is that there is no scriptural basis for their theology, so they have to live the lifestyle in public in order to validate their claims.

This obviously is a part of the ethical question of interpretation and revelation. If one's theological understanding of scripture is off-centered, then one's ethics based on that understanding will be off course as well.

What is the answer to these inroads of evangelical humanism that seem to have us surrounded? It is very simple: Take seriously the admonition that your attitude should be the same as that of Christ Jesus.[9]

When the Word of Faith movement's leaders, who through their own *revelation knowledge*, bring extrabiblical doctrines into the church, one must be prepared to respond correctly in accordance with God's revealed will in scripture.

Scores of scholars for years have spoken out. Those include Dr. Walter Martin, a charismatic theologian, and D. R. McConnell, also a charismatic and author of the recent book, "**A Different Gospel**", Michael Horton, a well-known Christian author, has addressed the doctrinal issues in his book, "**The Agony of Deceit**", as well.

As the issue is drawn into clearer focus, the reader needs to understand this is neither a *charismatic* nor a *non-charismatic* issue. It is an issue of biblical truth and accountability to that truth versus heretical doctrines.

If anything has been learned about the recent scandals of modern televangelists which could be summed up in one word, that one word would be *accountability* (or lack thereof).

That word, more than any other, has surfaced and has been expressed by both the secular public and the body of Christ as a desperate desire to bring some kind of reform to the practices of certain popular TV preachers.

Most of the outcry has been as a result of the immoral conduct and lack of financial accountability on the part of Christian leaders who were supposed to be examples of clean Christian character.

Christians are to hold one another accountable for one another's behavior (1 John 3:17; Galatians 6:2; Titus 1:9; 1 Timothy 1:3,4; 4:16; II Timothy 4:2; Matthew 18:15-16). There is no doubt about being "thy brother's keeper"! However, the fact that seems to escape most Christians is this: a person's actions are the result of their beliefs. A person lives a certain way because a person believes a certain way. Doctrine frames behavior.

Christians are to be accurate and balanced when giving criticism. One cannot stand idly by in silence when a person or group that claims to be Christian and yet seriously departs from the historical biblical doctrines of orthodox Christianity,. (Matt. 18:15-

16). To not speak out would be dishonoring to God and unloving, not only to Christians, but also to the propagators of the error.

It is common for the word-faith teachers to warn, "touch not the Lord's anointed", meaning that one cannot criticize or question in any way the Word of Faith teachers and what they are teaching. Some of the Evangelical Humanist teachers have said to do so carries serious consequences.

For example, the Christian Research Institute has documented that John Avanzini, along with TBN's Paul Crouch have said the reason Walter Martin died is God killed him because he spoke out against them. The implication is "that's what will happen to anyone who does speak out against them."[10]

It seems that if one disputes these leaders' words or deeds it is equivalent to questioning God Himself. Those who advocate such authority assume that Scripture supports their view.

They point to biblical proof texts such as Psalm 105:15, "Touch not mine anointed, and do my prophets no harm" (KJV). If one looks at the passage, it will reveal that it has nothing to do with questioning the teachings of church leaders.

In the Old Testament, the phrase, "the Lord's anointed", is used to refer to the kings of Israel (I Samuel 12:35; 24:6, 10, 16, 23; II Samuel 1:14, 16; 19:21; Psalms 10:6), and not to prophets. In the context of Psalms 105 the reference is to patriarchs in general (vv. 8-15; ef, I Chronicles 16:15-22).

Psalms 105:15 has nothing to do with the issue of questioning the teachings of any of God's "anointed". In the context of this passage, the words "touch" and "do harm" have to do with inflicting physical harm upon someone.

Specifically, in I Sam. 24:6, the phrase "touch not the Lord's anointed" refers to David's refraining from killing King Saul when he had the opportunity. It means in that context, "not to kill".

The fact is David did rebuke Saul publicly more than once and called him to account for his actions before God. He said in I Sam.

24:12, "The Lord judge between me and thee, but mine hands shall not be upon thee".

If this *"touch not"* mentality is applied in the way that the Evangelical Humanist leaders say, then it could also be argued that no one who claims to be a spokesman for God should be called to account for what he or she teaches.

No one would be rebuked and one would have to accept the teachings of all who claim to be Christian, including Joseph Smith and Mormonism, the Jehovah's Witnesses, and the Watchtower Society. Virtually all teachings, whether cultic or not, would be credible. The truth is that nobody's teachings or practices are beyond biblical judgment, especially those who are seen as leaders.

What allows Christians to claim Joseph Smith is a false teacher? It is not the fact that he claimed to speak "revelation knowledge". It is because one examines the doctrine in comparison to the Bible. Doctrine must be the means of measurement.

Recently, I made a list of Scripture texts in the New Testament that warn against, or refute, error. Though the list is not exhaustive by any means, it shows that such texts are found in every book of the New Testament except Philemon. In Matthew 7:15 Jesus warns against false prophets. In Mark 13:5,6 and Luke 21:8 Jesus warns us against false christs.

The New Testament deals with heresy in two ways, negatively and positively. Negatively it warns against and exposes it. Positively, it teaches, explains, and presents the truth as a counter to some error affecting the Church.

Christians are not called to render a condemning judgment upon anyone (for that alone is in God's hands), but are to render a discerning judgment upon all teachings. It is important for Christians to test all things by the scripture as the Bereans did when they examined the words of the Apostle Paul (Acts 17:11, I Thes. 5:2). The Bible is useful for correcting and rebuking, as well as for preaching and teaching (II Timothy 4:2).

Additionally, this is not a question of whether God has used these men in the salvation of many people. If and when the gospel is preached, "it is the power of God unto salvation to every one that believeth" (Romans 1:16). The problem is unbiblical doctrine which corrupts the essential Biblical teaching of the person and work of Christ.

It has not been easy to write this article, because the issue is sensitive. There are many sincere, committed Christians following these teachers, sometimes not even realizing what is being taught. It is also a crucial issue. It is not a threat from outside the church; it is a growth from within. Spiritual surgery, which is long overdue, is needed to stop it from spreading further. The Body of Christ must speak out.[11]

---

[1] THE AMPLIFIED NEW TESTAMENT, from The Amplified Bible, Expanded Edition, (Zondervan Corporation and The Lockman Foundation: La Habra, CA: 1987)

[2] Elwood McQuaid, "Before the Alter of 'I'," MOODY MONTHLY, November, 1986

[3] Kenneth Copeland, THE LAWS OF PROSPERITY, (np: Broken Arrow, OK), p. 104. np.

[4] Kenneth Hagin, "Zoe: The God-Kind of Life," 1989. pp. 35-36, 41

[5] Napoleon Hill, GROW RICH WITH PEACE OF MIND, (Ballantine Books: 1987), pp. 215-219.

[6] Napoleon Hill, QUOTES TO INSPIRE YOU, http://www.cybernation.com/victory/quotations/authors/quotes_hill_napoleon.html

[7] Dr. Charles Farah, Jr., Pneuma: The Journal of the Society for Pentecostal Studies, "A Critical Analysis: The "Roots and Fruits" of Faith-Formula Theology" (Spring, 1981, pp. 3-21}

[8] H. Terris Newman, Pneuma: The Journal of the Society for Pentecostal Studies, (Spring 1990, pp. 32-55)

[9] Philippians 2:5

[10] Quote used on the "Bible Answer Man" broadcast from the Spring 1990 "Praise-A-Thon" on TBN

[11] Clete Hux Accountability: The Way to Touch God's Anointed (Watchman Fellowship. http://www.watchman.org/reltop/). Vol. 10, No. 3, 1993

7

THE CONSEQUENCES

The most obvious result of this doctrine is the belief that Christians should live successful lives after the standards of the American image of success. Most prominent examples of this would include Jim and Tammy Bakker and Oral and Richard Roberts.

The Bakkers said the reason for their affluent lifestyle was they wanted to be better bait. Their better bait consisted of a mansion at their theme park, Heritage USA, a new $600,000 home in Palm Springs, $265,000 in hush money to mute word of a single sexual encounter in Florida in 1980, a Rolls Royce, flashy clothes, and jewelry as well as millions of dollars to use as they pleased, in the form of a large salary and exorbitant bonuses. Yet it may well have been the bait that brought them down. Very few men can handle the feeling of power and indestructibility that comes with wealth.[1] Hebrews 13:4-5 says "*⁴ Marriage is honourable in all, and the bed undefiled: but whoremongers and adulterers God will judge. ⁵ Let your conversation be without covetousness; and be content with such things as ye have: for He hath said, I will never leave thee, nor forsake thee.*" (KJV) What these verses are saying is, "Let your marriage be held in honor among all, and let the marriage bed be undefiled' for fornicators and adulterers will be judged by God. Let your way of life be free from the love of money and be content with what you have.

One commentator put it this way:

> "Greed of gain and sexual impurity are often joined in life, for one aids and abets the other. Paul therefore, warned that 'For the love of money is the root of all evil' 1 Tim 6:10a (KJV) The possession of wealth often opens opportunity for sensual indulgence which otherwise might not be present. . ."[2]

Oral Roberts went to his prayer tower in a successful attempt to raise eight million dollars (with the help of a Florida dog track owner) with a statement that God told him that He would kill him if the funds were not raised by a certain deadline. During this same time his son, Richard, was moving into a two-story mansion complete with a large swimming pool in the back yard. Besides their homes in the Tulsa area, both Oral and Richard have expensive homes in Palm Springs, California.[3]

These events bring an embarrassment to the cause of Christ in our world. Those who are already skeptical about trusting in Christ are given another excuse to use to fend off attempts to witness to them.

This writer has had many people in his life who have said things like, "What's your friend Jim Bakker doing these days?" or "If that is Christianity then I don't want anything to do with it."

By far the most important consequences are the effect this false teaching has upon the unsuspecting believer. An unwarranted sense of guilt can be a devastating result. When one begins to realize they are not meeting the unrealistic standards of their teachers, they often turn away from faith entirely. This writer has often dealt with people who have a sense of disillusionment as a result of their inability to have "enough faith" to make the things happen they want to happen.

When this writer was a pastor he had multiple encounters with those who were involved with this teaching. At one time a young couple almost succumbed to this error. They had a newborn child who was diagnosed with juvenile diabetes. A friend of theirs was involved with the Hagin Rehma Church in Broken Arrow, Oklahoma. The friend urged them to stop giving the baby insulin. They were told that if they continued to give the insulin to the baby that they were showing a lack of faith in his healing. It took many weeks of counseling with this couple before they realized that if they had taken the "friend's" advice, their child probably would have died. Today, that child is a strapping healthy young man. He still takes his insulin faithfully, watches his diet, and exercises regularly. He honors God with a life lived for Him.[4] Hobart Freeman's Faith Assembly Church is a classic example of what can happen when people take these teachings to their ultimate end. Over 100 died as a result.[5]

This writer would challenge you to NEVER place your faith in any man or his teachings other than Christ Himself. The apostle Paul once wrote:

> "⁶ I marvel that ye are so soon removed from him that called you into the grace of Christ unto another gospel: ⁷ Which is not another; but there be some that trouble you, and would pervert the gospel of Christ. ⁸ But though we, or an angel from heaven, preach any other gospel unto you than that which we have preached unto you, let him be accursed. ⁹ As we said before, so say I now again, If any *man* preach any other gospel unto you than that ye have received, let him be accursed.
>
> ¹⁰ For do I now persuade men, or God? or do I seek to please men? for if I yet pleased men, I should not be the servant of Christ. ¹¹ But I certify you, brethren, that the gospel which was preached of me is not after man. ¹² For I neither received it of man, neither was I taught *it,* but by the revelation of Jesus Christ." Gal 1:6-12 (KJV)

Paul here warns us of this other gospel. The original Greek word here is HETEROS. It is used in Phil. 3:15, "otherwise (minded)," i.e., "differently minded.[6] There is little in what we have seen that even resembles the Gospel of Jesus Christ our Lord and Savior. They certainly are not likeminded with proper interpretation of Scripture. The clear Gospel has been perverted in order to "please men".

It is pleasing to men's ears to tell them that they can have anything they want whenever they want. It would be an easy thing to be drawn into this heresy if one were not thoroughly grounded in what the word of God really says.

Two thousand years ago, Paul wrote to pastor-teacher Timothy with regard to this very subject—the Christian and material possessions. He spoke of those " ⁵ Perverse disputings of men of corrupt minds, and destitute of the truth, <u>supposing that gain is godliness</u>: from such <u>withdraw thyself</u>. [APHISTEMI *draw away from, shun, flee from*] [7] ⁶ But <u>godliness with contentment</u> AUTARKEIA *1) a perfect condition of life in which no aid or support is needed 2) sufficiency of the necessities of life 3) a mind contented with its lot, contentment]*[8] is great gain. ⁷ For we brought nothing into *this* world, *and it is* certain we can carry nothing out. ⁸ And having food and raiment let us be therewith content. ⁹ But they that will be rich fall into temptation and a snare, and *into* many foolish and hurtful lusts, which drown men in destruction and perdition. ¹⁰ For the love of money is the root of all evil: which while <u>some coveted after</u> [OREGOMAI *to stretch one's self out in order to touch or to grasp something, to reach after or desire something*],[9] <u>they have erred</u> [APOPLANAO> *is translated "seduce" in Mark 13:22 (RV, "lead astray")*] [10] from the faith, and pierced themselves through with many sorrows. ¹¹ But thou, O man of God, <u>flee these things</u> [pheugo> *"to flee" (Lat., fuga, "flight," etc.; cp. Eng. "fugitive, subterfuge"), is rendered "escape" in Matt. 23:33; Heb. 11:34— Vine's Expository Dictionary of Old and New Testament Words]*[11]; and follow after righteousness, godliness, faith, love, patience, meekness." 1 Tim 6:5-11 (KJV)

This is a clear refutation of the popular, ear-tickling "Prosperity Message," and therefore, a very important passage for our day, as it was in Timothy's. Think about this:

> We [Christians] are to be "content" with our material possessions. This is the opposite of being "eager" for money, which is equated with "the love of money." The word "eager" (verse 10) means: "reach out after, covet after, desire." **This speaks of greed, another name for idolatry (Col. 3:5; Eph. 5:5). Remember, ALL idolaters will end up in the fiery lake of burning sulfur (Rev. 21:8)!** Therefore, a very real DANGER—namely the fiery lake of burning sulfur—exists through any message, including this one, which would generate the love of money! Furthermore, some do wander from the faith because of such a teaching and have been plunged into ruin and destruction, verses 9 and 10! The same Greek word as found here in verse 9 is also used in Matt. 7:13 and rendered "destruction" which clearly

refers to Hell: ". . . For wide is the gate and broad is the road that leads to destruction, and many enter through it."

As a safeguard against this, Paul advises the people of God to flee from the desire to get rich and instead pursue much more important things like righteousness, godliness, faith, love, endurance, and gentleness. Consequently, the real issues evolve around Christian goals, ambitions and priorities. They are to be spiritual and eternal, not material and temporal; yet we are to provide for our relatives and family (1 Tim. 5:8)!

Paul identifies those who teach a message that generates a love for money as people who "have been robbed of the truth," verse 5. **This is a blanket statement. Regardless of any signs and wonders some may be able to perform or alleged visits from Jesus Christ Himself as they claim!**

Those who promote this false "name it and claim it" doctrine teach each other and as they do, the cycle of deception deepens. The perversion of the truth becomes more and more blatant. It is akin to spiritual inbreeding with corresponding problems in the doctrinal areas that physical inbreeding brings on in the natural.

One must make certain that he believes the Gospel as it was delivered by Matthew, Mark, Luke, John, Peter, Paul, Titus, James and Jude. These are the men who were inspired by God's Holy Spirit to deliver His truths to us. John made it very clear in the closing verses of Revelation that God's Word was complete, that nothing more should be added. He wrote, "[18] For I testify unto every man that heareth the words of the prophecy of this book, If any man shall add unto these things, God shall add unto him the plagues that are written in this book: [19] And if any man shall take away from the words of the book of this prophecy, God shall take away his part out of the book of life, and out of the holy city, and *from* the things which are written in this book." Revelation 22:18-19 (KJV)

> "Beloved, believe not every spirit, but try the spirits whether they are of God: because many false prophets are gone out into the world."
> 1 John 4:1 (KJV)

---

[1] Lewis J. Lord, et. al., "an Unholy War in the TV Pulpits," US.NEWS AND WORLD REPORT, April 6. 1987, pp. 59, 65

[2] THE BROADMAN BIBLE COMMENTARY, (Broadman Press: Nashville), vol. 12, p. 93, 1970

[3] Lord, p. 58

[4] BJ Hall, Personal Counseling Sessions

[5] See INTRODUCTION to this document, p. 4

[6] VINE'S EXPOSITORY DICTIONARY OF OLD AND NEW TESTAMENT WORDS, v.s. "heteros"

[7] STRONGS GREEK AND HEBREW DICTIONARY, s.v. "aphistemi"

[8] STRONGS GREEK AND HEBREW DICTIONARY, s.v. "autarkeia"

[9] STRONGS GREEK AND HEBREW DICTIONARY, s.v. "oregomai"

[10] Vine's Expository Dictionary of Old and New Testament Words, s.v. "apoplanao"

[11] STRONGS GREEK AND HEBREW DICTIONARY, s.v. "pheugo"

BIBLIOGRAPHY

BIBLE

All references are from the King James Version of the Bible.

Acts 1:8

Genesis 3:5

Hebrews 13:4-5

Luke 6:24

Luke 9:58

Matthew 4:1-4

Matthew 28:18-20

Philippians 2:5

I Timothy 6:17

BOOKS

Capps, Charles, GOD'S CREATIVE POWER, (np: England, Arkansas, nd)

Capps, Charles, THE TONGUE—A CREATIVE FORCE. (np: England, Arkansas, nd).

Copeland, Kenneth, THE LAWS OF PROSPERIETY, (np: Broken Arrow, Oklahoma, nd).

Freeman, Hobart POSITIVE THINKING AND CONFESSION (Faith Publications, nd)

Hagin, Kenneth E., BIBLE STUDY FAITH COURSE, (np: Broken Arrow, Oklahoma, nd).

Hagin, Kenneth E., ZOE: THE GOD-KIND OF LIFE, (np: Broken Arrow, Oklahoma, 1989).

Hagin, Sr. Kenneth E., THE AUTHORITY OF THE BELIEVER, (np: Broken Arrow, Oklahoma, nd)

Hill, Napoleon, GROW RICH WITH PEACE OF MIND, (Ballantine Books, 1967)

Meyer, Joyce, *The Most Important Decision You Will Ever Make: A Complete And Thorough Understanding Of What It Means To Be Born Again* (Tulsa: Harrison House, 1991)

Wilkerson, David, A PROPHECY WALL OF FIRE, (World Challenge: Lindale, Texas, nd).

Williams, J. Rodman, ERA OF THE SPIRIT, (Logos International, Plainfield, New Jersey, 1971)

CONVERSATIONS AND INTERVIEWS

Campbell, Jim, Personal interview held July 17, 1987 in Mr. Campbell's home, Depew, Oklahoma

Hall, Connie, et. al., Personal conversation held June 17, 1987, Gore, Oklahoma

BJ Hall, et. al., Personal counseling sessions over thirty three years of pastoral ministry between 1969 and 2001

INTERNET RESOURCES

Napoleon Hill, QUOTES TO INSPIRE YOU, http://www.cybernation.com/victory/quotations/authors/quotes_hill_napoleon.html

Hux, Clete, Accountability: The Way to Touch God's Anointed (Watchman Fellowship. http://www.watchman.org/reltop/ . *Vol. 10, No. 3, 1993*

Pearson, Bishop Carlton D., JESUS: THE SAVIOR OF THE WORLD (The Gospel of Inclusion), http://www.myfaith.com/carlton-pearson-inclusion.htm

CAMBRIDGE ADVANCED LEARNER'S DICTIONARY, Online http://dictionary.cambridge.org/cald

LETTERS

Capps, Charles, Personal letter, June 4, 1982

Roberts, Oral, Partnership letter, September 16, 1980

Grant, W.V., Solicitation Letter, nd

PERIODICALS

Bjornstad, Dr. James, "What's Behind the Prosperity Gospel?" MOODY MONTHLY, (November 1986, p. 19)

CHRISTIANITY TODAY, (November 23, 1984)

Copeland, Kenneth, "Jesus - Our Lord of Glory", *Believer's Voice of Victory*, April, 1982.

Farah, Jr., Dr. Charles, PNEUMA: THE JOURNAL OF THE SOCIETY FOR PENTECOSTAL STUDIES, "A Critical Analysis: The "Roots and Fruits" of Faith-Formula Theology" (Spring, 1981,)

FOUNDATION MAGAZINE, Fundamental Evangelistic Association, Los Osos, California (Mar-Apr 2000)

Lord, Lewis J., et. al., "An Unholy War in the TV Pulpits," U.S. NEWS AND WORLD REPORT, (April 6, 1987)

McQuaid, Elwood, "Before the Alter of 'I'," MOODY MONTHLY, (November 1986)

Newman, H. Terris, PNEUMA: THE JOURNAL OF THE SOCIETY FOR PENTECOSTAL STUDIES, (Spring 1990)

Price, Frederick K.C., EVER INCREASING FAITH MESSENGER, (June 1990).

REFERENCE WORKS

THE AMPLIFIED NEW TESTAMENT, from The Amplified Bible, Expanded Edition, (Zondervan Corporation and The Lockman Foundation: La Habra, CA: 1987)

THE BROADMAN BIBLE COMMENTARY, (Broadman Press: Nashville, Tennessee: 1970)

Dake, Finis Jennings, DAKE'S ANNOTATED REFERENCE BIBLE, (Dake Bible Sales, inc.: Lawrenceville, Georgia: 1981)

DICTIONARY OF PENTECOSTAL AND CHARISMATIC MOVEMENTS, 1988.

Robertson, A.T., WORD PICTURES IN THE NEW TESTAMENT, (Broadman Press: Nashville Tennessee: 1932)

VINE'S EXPOSITORY DICTIONARY OF OLD AND NEW TESTAMENT WORDS

WEBSTER'S NEW COLLEGIATE DICTIONARY, 1977

TAPES TV AND RADIO BROADCASTS

Copeland, Kenneth, THE FORCES OF LOVE, tape #BCC-56, Broken Arrow, Oklahoma

Copeland, Kenneth, WHAT HAPPENED FROM THE CROSS TO THE THRONE? cassette tape, Kenneth Copeland Ministries, parenthesis mine

Hinn, Benny, Benny Hinn broadcast on TBN, December 15, 1990

KNYD-FM, Charles Capps, 21 July 1987

KNYD-FM, Dr. Daisey Osborn, "Women's Voice", 20 July 1987

Meyer, Joyce, GO TO THE UPPER ROOM AND WAIT (Audiotape 6).

Meyer, Joyce, WITCHCRAFT & RELATED SPIRITS (Audiotape, Part 1).

Meyer, Joyce, WHAT HAPPENED FROM THE CROSS TO THE THRONE?, (Audiotape that is mysteriously no longer available)

Meyer, Joyce, TROPHIES OF GOD'S GRACE (Audiotape, Part 1).

Avanzini, John, et. al. "Praise-A-Thon" on TBN, Quote used on the "Bible Answer Man" broadcast from the Spring 1990

ABOUT THE AUTHOR

John "BJ" Hall has been in the gospel ministry since 1969. He served first as a music and youth minister at First Baptist Church, Archadia, Oklahoma, followed by the same position at First Baptist Church, Disney, Oklahoma. In June of 1970, at the age of 19, he was bi-vocational pastor of Poyner Baptist Church near Southwest City Missouri. He was then pastor of First Baptist Church, Strang, Oklahoma. Following that, he began a series of full time pastoral positions in Adair, Webbers Falls, Depew and Sapulpa, all in northeastern Oklahoma. In January of 2001, BJ answered God's call on his life to full time evangelism. He is a member of the Oklahoma Conference of Southern Baptist Evangelists, and serves as Deacon and Sunday School Teacher at Canyon Road Baptist Church, Tulsa, Oklahoma when he is not "Out preach'n and sing'n for the Lord."

Made in the USA
Charleston, SC
01 December 2011